Motorcycles

by Ellen Kahaner

Capstone Press

P.O. Box 669, Mankato, MN, U.S.A. 56002-0669

CAPSTONE PRESS
818 North Willow Street • Mankato, Minnesota 56001

Printed in the United States of America.

Library of Congress Cataloging-in-Publication Data
Kahaner, Ellen.
    Motorcycles / Ellen Kahaner.
    p. cm. -- (Cruisin')
    Summary: Describes the history and characteristics of motorcycles, how they are made, how they work, and their varied uses. Also discusses important racing competitions.
    ISBN 1-56065-070-2
    1. Motorcycles--Juvenile literature. [1. Motorcycles. 2. Motorcycle racing.] I. Title. II. Series.
TL440.K32 1990
629.227'5--dc20

                                            89-39673
                                               CIP
                                                AC

Photo credits
American Motorcyclist: 8, 18, 22, 30, 32, 34, 37, 38, 45, 46
Harley-Davidson Inc.: 4, 6, 10, 12, 14, 17, 24, 28, 36, 42-44, 48
American Honda Motor Company: 20, 24, 26, 36, 40, 47

Contents

Introduction 5

What Makes a Motorcycle Work 19

Production: From Factory
   to Showroom 23

Custom Styling 29

Racing Competitions 31

Special and Everyday Uses 39

Motorcycles of Tomorrow 41

To Learn More 43

Glossary 47

1903 "factory." Birthplace of the first three Harley-Davidsons.

1903 model, one of three produced in the first year's production run.

Introduction

The First Motorcycles

More than one hundred years ago, the first motorcycles bumped down the road. These bikes had three wheels. Their engines ran on steam. In the 1860s, the first two-wheel bike was made in France. This bike also had a steam engine. It took a long time to start and was not very strong. Imagine how hot it was to sit over an engine that needed boiling water to run!

The first successful combustion engine was built in Germany by Nikolaus Otto and Eugen Langen in 1866. This engine led the way to the modern motorcycle. At first designers could not agree where to put the engine. Some even tried putting it behind the bike on its own little wheel. In 1901, the first bike with a motor between the wheels was sold. This basic layout is still used.

The Modern Bike

Today, motorcycles are sophisticated and powerful machines. They are made very much like cars, except they have fewer parts.

All kinds of people ride motorcycles all over the world. Cycles are made in America, Japan, Germany, Italy and England. There are many types of

motorcycles. There are touring, sport, and cruiser or custom bikes, trailbikes, dual purpose, and racers.

Touring Bikes

Touring bikes are the biggest and heaviest bikes you can get. They have big engines. They're made for travel on the open road. A popular feature is "cruise control." This device holds the bike at a steady speed for long distances. There's room for a passenger and luggage. You can add lots of extras like stereo speakers, CB radios, even a computer.

Sport Bikes

Sport bikes are smaller, lighter and faster than touring bikes. They have many of the features of racing bikes. The best or "top of the line" sport bikes are called "superbikes." Superbikes have the largest engines and the most power.

Cruiser Bikes

Cruiser or custom bikes are built lean and low. Style is most important. They are good for short trips.

Trailbikes

Trail or dirtbikes are built to ride off paved roads. Often they do not require a license plate. They have special knobby tires to grip muddy ground.

The exhaust pipe is high set. This protects it from the rough turf. Long shock absorbers make the ride feel less bumpy. Trail bikers enjoy endurance races and obstacle course riding.

Dual Purpose bikes

Dual purpose bikes are part street, part dirt bikes. They are built to handle street riding as well as rough roads and dirt paths. A dual-purpose bike is good for someone who lives in a town near wooded areas. They are built with a lot of ground clearance. This means that if you pushed down on the seat, it would lower 5-6 inches toward the ground. On a sport bike, the seat would only lower 3 inches. More ground clearance gives you a smoother ride over rough roads.

Racing Bikes

Racers are built to reach high speeds fast. They have powerful engines. They are best for cornering. This means they can turn corners without loss of control. They are used at the race track.

No matter which bike you favor, you will want to know how it is designed. What makes an engine run? How are bikes made? What materials are used? What can the riders do to 'custom style' their own bike? These are some of the questions that will be answered in this book. You will also learn what equipment you need to ride a motor-

cycle safely and how motorcycles are used in racing competitions.

Motorcycle Design

Motorcycle designers or stylists are the people who design the bikes you see on the street, at the race track and on the open highway.

Louie Netz is a motorcycle designer. He heads the Styling Department at Harley-Davidson, Inc. in Milwaukee, Wisconsin. Harley-Davidson is the oldest motorcycle company in the U.S. Since 1903, they've made the "big" bikes you see on the road. Netz is a rider himself. He has been riding for over 15 years. This is important to being a good designer. There's nothing like real experience to give you ideas on how to improve things. He also watches what other people are riding and the ways they **customize** their bikes. Netz goes to motorcycle rallies. These rallies are held throughout the year all over the U.S. He talks to riders to find out what changes they want, and then he takes their suggestions back to the designers.

Model Making

Netz meets with the styling group at Harley-Davidson to talk over new ideas. The designers sit behind drawing boards where they sketch their ideas. Next they make a mock-up or model

motorcycle. The models are the size of an actual motorcycle and are made of brown clay. Clay is used so when a designer wants to make a change, more clay can be added or taken off the model. For that reason, clay models are used instead of wooden models.

Before the model is made, the clay is warmed in an oven to 105-110 degrees Fahrenheit. This makes the clay soft. Then the designers apply the clay to a form called a buck. The buck is made of wood or styrofoam. After the clay is applied to the buck, it has to cool to room temperature, about 72-75 degrees Fahrenheit. Then the designers begin to carve the clay.

Special tools must be used for clay modeling. These include rakes, cutting tools, and slicks. Slicks are two steel sheets that are very easy to move through the clay. Slicks are used to cut away chunks of clay. They can make a precise surface. The designers model the clay until it is exactly the right shape.

When the clay model is smooth, it can be primed or painted. Primer is applied to help protect the smooth clay surface. When the primer dries, the designers sand it, prime it, and sand it again until the model looks real. Once the designers are finished with their model, they turn it over to the

Engineering Department. The engineers must try to design the model into a machine that will work.

Engineering

The designers work closely with the engineers. The engineers draw the exact size and shape of each part of the new bike on paper. Each engineer works in an office at a drawing board. Engineers also draw with computers. The computers can show pictures in 3 dimensions or all sides of the bike.

Major style changes, like where the engine should be located on the bike, can take 18 months to 2 years to design. Simple design changes, like making the gas tank wider or thinner, can take 6 months.

Then the engineers go back to the designers. The designers work out the dimensions on paper, creating a test model. The second model is then made into a real motorcycle or working model.

Testing

The new bike must pass two tests to see if it works well and if it is a safe, sound bike. In a **durability test**, the bike is tested on the road. In a **structure** (stress) **test**, the part or piece is tested in a research development laboratory.

Durability Tests

Durability testing for Harley-Davidson takes place in Talladega, Alabama. The tests are held at a race track. Highly sophisticated packs are attached to the rider and to the cycle. These packs are monitored by a computer in a van that follows along. The results of the tests are given back to the Engineering Department.

Structure Tests

Structure or stress tests examine a single new part. The test is done in a research development laboratory. Harley-Davidson's laboratory is in Milwaukee, Wisconsin. A piece of metal or a spring might be pounded a million times in the laboratory to see how it will withstand use on the road.

The results of these tests are given back to engineering. The engineers decide whether the part is something they want to keep or to change. If they decide to keep the new part, the Manufacturing Department is contacted. If they decide to change the part it goes back to the drawing board or the part is scrapped altogether.

What Makes A Motorcycle Work

Engines are the source of power for motorcycles. Like cars and trucks, motorcycles have internal combustion engines. Internal combustion engines burn fuel (a mixture of gas and air) inside a cylinder. A cylinder is like a tube. In the cylinder are one or more solid cylinder-shaped pistons. A piston moves up and down many times every second.

How An Engine Works

When an engine is turned on, gas and air enter the cylinder. The pistons go to work, squeezing fuel to the top of the cylinder. The piston hits against a spark plug at the top of the cylinder. The spark plug sparks the fuel. This spark or small explosion pushes the piston down the cylinder. At the bottom of the cylinder is a rod which is attached to a crankshaft. When the piston moves down the cylinder, the rod turns the crankshaft. The crankshaft turns and this powers the cycle's rear wheel. In a matter of seconds, the engine is running.

What makes one cycle faster than another? The more cylinders, the faster and smoother the ride. Motorcycles can have one to four cylinders. The

smallest engine has one cylinder. The BMW R100S has twin cylinders. The Suzuki GT 750 has three cylinders. The Honda Gold Wing has four. The engines are designed to keep the weight low in the frame for better control.

Engine Size

Motorcycle engines can be two, four, or six-stroke designs. A **stroke** is the number of times the piston moves up and down in the cylinder between each spark. A six-stroke engine is one in which the piston moves up and down six times between each spark. Most motorcycles today have six-stroke engines. They are stronger and cause less air pollution than other engines.

The size of an engine is measured by cubic centimeters ("ccs"). The larger the number of ccs the more powerful the engine. A street bike can be 50 ccs. In the United States, bikes are often 100-150 ccs to 1000 ccs or more. The Honda Gold Wing has 1500 ccs. It has as much power or pull as the family car. It can climb a steep hill or carry a lot of luggage.

Today's bikes are so sophisticated that many have their own microcomputers. A microcomputer is a small quarter inch computer. These control the timing of the ignition and amount of gas the bike uses.

Production: From Factory To Showroom

Motorcycles have many parts. These parts are put together in a factory. Some of these parts are produced by special suppliers. Some parts are made in the factory. Assembly line machines put many of these parts together. While machines and assembly lines speed up production, a lot of the work is done by human hands. A big cycle plant makes about 250 bikes a day.

At Harley-Davidson, engines and transmissions are built in a machine shop in Milwaukee, Wisconsin. These are shipped by truck to a warehouse in York, Pennsylvania. The engines and transmissions are taken from the warehouse to the factory. The factory in York covers one million square feet. The bikes are made in a "jelly bean system." This means that all different colors and models are produced at the same time.

The parts are put together in different stations or assembly areas of the factory. There are 66 stations.

The Wheel Station

The wheels are assembled at one station. The front and rear wheels are hung on a conveyor belt. The spokes get "trued up." This means the spokes are lined up correctly. The spoked wheels get laced. The laces are metal for extra strength.

The Press Station

While the wheels are being assembled, other stations are hard at work. At the press station, the gas tank and fenders are being formed out of big metal sheets. The metal is shaped by a machine called a press.

The Machine Center

A machine that does many operations is called a "**machining center**." This machine may be run by a computer. For example, a machining center mills, drills, and taps metal clamps into shape.

The completed parts are hung on racks. They are polished. Some of the parts are chrome plated. This means a thin layer of chrome is applied to the part. Chrome is the best weatherproofer there is. It prevents rust. The parts are polished again and painted with a spray gun. They are ready to be put on the bare frame. The frame is often made of round steel tubing. Steel tubing is easy to cut and strong. Sometimes aluminum is used because it is light weight.

It takes four hours to put all the parts on the bike. Some of the parts, like the exhaust pipe, are welded onto the bike. This means the part is joined to the bike with heat. When the bike is completed, it is roller tested. This is a test done in the factory. The gears, lights, horn, speedometer, wheels, and motor are checked. Then the bikes are lined up. One more part needs to be put on. It is the seat. Now the bikes are ready to be shipped.

The bikes are packed into wood crates. The crates are shipped to dealers. There the bikes will be displayed to customers in showrooms. For overseas transport, the bikes are **containerized**. This means the cycles are placed in 20 to 40-foot metal trailers. They're hitched onto a tractor which is then taken to a ship. When the ship gets to its destination, the trailers are lifted off the ship's deck by big cranes. They reach their final home by truck.

Honda's manufacturing plant in Marysville, Ohio, manufactures bikes that are sold in the United States and shipped to 15 countries. Honda also imports bikes from their factory in Japan to the U.S.

Custom Styling

When bikes arrive at a dealer's showroom, they are factory-assembled. This means they are ready to ride.

Sometimes riders like to add to and change the look of the bike. This is called customizing. Customizing can be done by riders, a dealer or a customizer. Riders can buy kits with special attachments. Extra lights and fancy saddlebags can be added to the bike. Some riders do their own paint jobs or add decals. Riders can even add stereo speakers for the passenger and CB radios.

Some customized bikes even become famous. Elizabeth Taylor, the actress, was given a bike by businessman Malcolm Forbes. The bike was called "Purple Passion" after Ms. Taylor's line of perfume. It was painted purple. The words "Purple Passion" were painted on the cycle.

The Bebop Bamboozle was one of 107 Harley-Davidson bikes featured at the halftime show on Superbowl 23 in 1989. This bike was custom-painted white. It had a fringed white leather seat and saddlebags with silver studs.

Have you ever seen a customized bike? If you owned a bike, how would you customize it?

Racing Competitions

The first motorcycle race was held on September 20, 1896. It was run between Paris, France and Nantes, France and covered 254 miles. Today, there are many kinds of motorcycle races. There are international, national, and local competitions. They are held on dirt tracks and drag strips. There are team races and individual races. Races are held all over this country and worldwide.

Trailbikes

Trailbikes are used in **motocross** races. These races are held indoors on rough tracks. Races are run in different classes depending on engine size. Motocross is popular on the West Coast.

Trailbikes are also used for endurance races known as trials. These races cover a tough and demanding course. Sometimes trailbikes may "race" at a walking pace through water, woods, and over steep hills. This kind of racing requires great balance. One reason is that the riders are not allowed to put their feet on the ground for support. Even if they come to a stop, trial racing rules require riders to keep their feet on the pegs. Imagine riding around a tree or going up a wet

rock slide and not putting your feet down to steady yourself.

International Six Day Trials are held in Europe. In this race, riders are timed over 5,280 miles. Some of the riding requires quick reflexes and turns around tight corners. Trials are held in the United States on the East Coast.

Grand Prix Racing

The Grand Prix Race is not just one race, but a series of races. Riders travel from all over the world to compete in Grand Prix races. Riders are sponsored by factory or company teams. It's too expensive for a single rider to compete without financial support. Grand Prix bikes are custom made. The racing bikes are developed in company research laboratories. Later on, ideas tried out in racing bikes are used on factory-made bikes.

The world championship is determined by the winners of these races. There are 15 races held all over the world from March through September. These races are held for different sized engines. The most important race is for the 500cc bikes. The larger the number of ccs, the larger the engine. The winner in this class is the World Champion. The winner of the Grand Prix rides in 15 different races.

At the end of the season all the points are totaled. The highest total wins the Championship.

Sidecars

Years ago, sidecar frames were bolted or clamped to the motorcycle frame. Sidecars now look like something out of a science fiction movie. Some sidecars even have roofs. In sidecar races, the passenger sits next to the rider and plays an important part. The passenger throws his or her weight to balance when turning corners. The sidecar and motorcycle are constructed as one piece. It is built close to the ground and as streamlined as possible. This design allows the wind to pass smoothly and not slow the machine. These racers can go up to 256 miles an hour.

Racers Or Superbikes

Superbike races are commonly known as drag races. Racers or superbikes, the fastest of bikes, compete against each other. These bikes are made to cover a quarter of a mile in the least amount of time. Drag racing is a very popular sport in the United States. Races are held on the same race tracks as drag races for cars.

Street bikes and custom bikes race against each other. Street bikes have to meet strict safety standards. Riders have to wear the proper racing gear. Some bikes can be completely custom made.

Bikes compete with other bikes having the same size engines. There's one exception. In the top class, there's an unlimited category. This means that the engine can be any size, use any kind of fuel or any number of **turbo** chargers. A turbo engine has a pump that takes every bit of extra fuel and air back into the engine. Speed is everything. There's even a rocket-powered bike that can reach a speed of 200 miles per hour in 7 seconds.

Special and Everyday Uses

Special Uses

Motorcycles were used in World War I and World War II. During World War I, bikes were used for scouting and to carry messages. In World War II, motorcycle troops were called Iron Ponies. These were the fastest land army troops in the war.

Motorcycles are used by many law enforcement departments. They are used to escort cars carrying important people. They keep traffic moving in busy cities and help to fight crime. Police forces use bikes that have sirens and warning lights like police cars.

Everyday Uses

Motorcycles are a good way to get to work or school. A side car can carry extra passengers. For vacations, with a hitch on the back, camping gear can come along. Bikes are made to be used for many different purposes.

Motorcycles of Tomorrow

Looking into the future is fun. New ideas are tested on the race track before going into mass production. So a look into the future means a trip to the race track. Racers used radial tires first. Three-cylinder engines and aluminum frames were used at the Grand Prix by Honda before they were put into touring bikes.

Today, low, light Grand Prix racing bikes with no frames and carbon-fiber bodywork are the most modern machines in motorcycle design. These futuristic-looking frames will be found on tomorrow's cycles.

Motorcycle designers are moving away from their basic pedal-bike roots. Front steering forks now steer the front wheel. They will be replaced by "hub-centered steering." This means the front wheel will pivot or turn on bearings in its hub that are linked to the handlebars. More lightweight metals like aluminum and more plastics will be used inside the engine. New ceramics for use as bearings may mean that engines can run without oil.

Now most riders use their feet to control the gears. In the future, automatic gearboxes will become a common feature. Tires will have to get wider as bikes get faster. Plastic tires to replace rubber ones are even being tested! Brakes will change to meet the needs of bikes at greater speeds. What is strange today will seem ordinary tomorrow.

To Learn More

You have just been introduced to the world of motorcycles. There is so much more you can learn! If you want to learn more about how a motorcycle is put together, there are many model-making kits available. You can build a classic model or a racer.

Cycling magazines will keep you up to date with the motorcycling world. You can also look at back issues of magazines on your favorite subjects at the library. For sport biking and racing, check out <u>Cycle World</u>, <u>Motorcyclist</u>, and <u>Cycle</u>. For touring, look at <u>Rider</u>.

Most libraries have books on motorcycling. You can learn more about the history of motorcycling, motorcycles around the world, racing, record breakers, and how a motorcycle works. A book published at the end of every year is <u>Motocourse</u>. It will give you information about the racing scene. It primarily covers road racing and events in Europe.

Another way to get information is to go on a factory tour with your class or visit a dealer's show-room. Many communities have motorcycle clubs. You can find out the names and phone numbers from local motorcycle dealers. Clubs can give you information on rallies and special events in your area. And you can write to the Motorcycle Safety Foundation (2 Jenner Street, Suite 150, Irvine, California 92718) for cycle safety information. The more you know, the better!

Glossary

Containerizing: The process of putting motorcycles in metal trailers for overseas shipment.

Customized: A motorcycle with special features that show the personality of its owner.

Durability Test: After a new motorcycle piece or part is designed and made, it is tested out for 'durability' on the road. (See Structure Test)

Machining Center: A computer controlled machine in the factory that performs more that one operation on a part. For example, a machining center mills, drills, and taps the clamps into shape.

Motocross: A type of race that takes place indoors, on a rough circuit.

Stroke: The number of times the piston moves up and down in the engine's cylinder between each spark. For example, in a six-stroke engine the piston moves up and down six times between each spark.

Structure Test: In addition to being durability tested, a new motorcycle piece or part is tested in a research laboratory under mock conditions. Sometimes called a Stress Test.

Turbo: An exhaust-driven pump that forces extra fuel and air into the engine.